Dr. Barbara L. Swinney

It's
Always
DEEPER

6 Step to Achieving Perpetual Success

PUBLISHING COMPANY

PUBLISHING COMPANY

P.O. Box 3401
Atlanta, Georgia

Copyright © 2018 by Dr. Barbara Swinney

Cover Design:
Michael Bray of Nidobrand

Book Design:
BSI Publishing Company

Permission granted to use stories by individuals
included for demonstration.

First printing: August 2018

It's Always DEEPER

ISBN 978-1-7-325-2530-6

Printed in the United States of America.

DEDICATION

God, I am eternally grateful. To my babies, Jhardé and Jemiah, many years will pass before you are able to understand the blessing that you are to me. I am grateful to both of you for keeping me grounded by unknowingly reminding me of my role and purpose in life. I am extremely thankful to God for thinking me worthy enough to send me the two of you. Please remember that Mommy loves you, believes in you, and is certain that you are gifts to the world.

To my nine brothers and sisters, thank you for setting the standard for how people should treat me. You are responsible for everything that is wrong with me, and everything that is right! I am so proud to be a color in the rainbow that never ends.

Table of Contents

ACKNOWLEDGMENTS

Every personal experience that I share in this book, I share from a place of healing, wholeness, and a sincere desire to help you get unstuck and eliminate the barriers that may be keeping you from living the life you want. Some of the content is sensitive in nature and the events not only profoundly impacted my life, but forever changed the life of my daughters. I wanted to be transparent with you and honor myself, however, it was also important to me to make sure that I support and respect my daughters in the process. Only after acquiring their blessing, did I share my truth—the truth about my experiences.

I would also like to take the opportunity to thank all of the people who allowed me to integrate their stories as demonstrations throughout my DEEPER Journey. Thank you Dr. Johnnetta McSwain, author of Rising Above the Scars, Ms. Wongalee Waller, School Secretary; Mr. Henry James, Classroom Teacher; and the Parents of Henry and Victor Groover. I am hopeful that your stories will help our readers live The DEEPER Life!

Introduction

It's *Always* DEEPER!

*Do you want your life to go higher? Then you have to go **D-E-E-P-E-R.*** This revelation slapped me right in the forehead early one Christmas morning.

Most of us could probably look into the corner of our lives and find some of our hopes and dreams buried under cobwebs and dust bunnies. At times we get stuck. This is exactly where my best friend Len was when she texted me early one Christmas morning requesting me to call her. As she illuminated the many pits of a failed relationship and talked about how she "could've, would've, should've" done something 7different, it became clear that Len's foot was stuck. After listening to her vent, I could not resist the urge to interrupt with a few choice words intended to nudge her back to center. Little did I know the very words that I spoke to her would turn on me; leading me on a journey of self-awareness and self-actualization. The DEEPER I went, the more determined I became to reach my goals and become who I wanted to be.

In this book, I will share with you some pivotal moments in my life and invite you to join me in using the **D-E-E-P-E-R.** Life Strategy— an intentional process for getting "unstuck" that will help you achieve perpetual success in every area of your life.

If there are any hopes, goals, or dreams that you have allowed to fade into the background, it is now time that you go DEEPER; get to the bottom of yourself and...

> ***D****ecide What You Want:* Clarify your vision and get clear about what you would like to accomplish.

Examine Your Life: Identify behaviors that have impeded your progress. Figure out why you do what you do.

Eliminate the Barriers: Replace negative behaviors with those that move you toward your goals and the life you want to live.

Make a Plan of Action: Determine the steps necessary to get what you want! Be specific and intentional in the action steps to accomplish your goals.

Evaluate Your Progress: Get honest with yourself regarding your progress. Celebrate and make adjustments as necessary.

Realize That You Can Do It!:   Apply these principles to your life and you WILL reach your goals and become who you want to be!

As you walk through this book, you will have the opportunity to reflect and journal your thinking in the **Deeper Thinking** sections at the end of each chapter. In your quiet time—Yes! You will need to make quiet time a part of your regular schedule give special attention to your current reality and consider where you would like to be.

Go ahead, grab a highlighter and a pen and let us get started. I cannot wait to share my **DEEPER** experience with you!

Chapter

1

Decide What You Want

Getting what you want requires one single, major step—decide.

~Dr. Barbara L. Swinney

My phone buzzed at 6:00 am; it was a text from a close friend. The text read: I know it is Christmas morning, but please call me when you get a chance.

Oh, no! Why would she send a text like this on Christmas morning? She must really need me! The house was silent. I knew my girls were still sleeping, so I had a few minutes to talk. I slid from under the covers, tiptoed out of the room, and gently closed the door so I would not wake my husband. I went to the basement in the laundry room. I just could not ignore the pile of dirty clothes on top of the washer, so I took a minute to throw a load in the machine. "OK…I shouldn't wake anyone from here." I muttered. I squatted on the step stool that sat in floor, rested my back against the washer, and dialed her number. She picked up, but did not say a word at first. I could hear her congested, stuffy-nosed breathing. After about forty-five seconds, with tears running down her face, a dry mouth, and a snotty nose. I had had the experience of her crying on my shoulder before and was quite familiar with the sound my distressed friend. See, Len and I were like sisters and had grown through much of our lives together; from our first elementary school crush, the "I-think-I'm-going-to-die" high school heartbreak, and meeting that college sweetheart, to marrying the "soul mate," the complications and joys of childbirth, losing a parent, and now…whatever she was planning to share with me during this call.

"He took the kids! It's Christmas morning and he took the kids!" I know her well and recognize that she has a tendency to exaggerate. So I took out my reality radar to assess whether we had a kidnapping on our hands or if there was something more logical at the root of this oak tree. Calmly, I queried, "What do you mean...did you agree to this?" She went on to explain the situation. It turned out that her recently estranged husband, who lived in another state, had brought the children to visit her so that they could spend Christmas Eve together as a family. He and the kids left on Christmas morning to return to his home state. I would do anything possible to demonstrate my support to a friend, but I became a bit agitated as I am hearing the drama emerge. Her children were in no danger, there were no threats of forbidding her to see her babies, and the tears and snot were just the result of a deeper, inner conflict of the simultaneous clinging and releasing of what once was. I took a cleansing breath, relaxed, and allowed her to continue to vent. I listened patiently as she dreadfully reached back to her past and pulled up all that she had hoped her relationship would be. It was clear that she was exasperated, pinned down by her own thoughts, and was looking for a lifeline to pull her out of what she and I fondly refer to as "crazyland". We depended on each other in that way—we would always, sometimes in unison, remind each other that, *We are all crazy, but once you recognize what crazy looks like, you can stop being crazy!*

Clearly, her foot was wedged in one of the cracks in the sidewalk in crazyland, and, in this moment, she did not have the mental or emotional fortitude to yank it out. I get it! Ending a relationship that you imagined lasting a lifetime, is a traumatic process. However, for quite some time, Len and I had committed to a spiritual journey together and had learned quite a bit about the pathology of human behavior that kept us locked in cyclical dysfunction. We learned the art of letting go and burying a "thing" after it dies. So after crying buckets of tears over a relationship that had been limp for some time, having numerous enlightening conversations, and experiencing several life coaching sessions together, I was sure we had evolved beyond this phase. We were OBVIOUSLY dealing with a setback!

Generally, I do a good job when it is my turn to be the rock, but this time I was just not in my best state of mind. So when I started to think—*Oh my goodness, we've been through all of this before!*—I felt a little guilty because Len had been there for me so many times; especially when I was experiencing my own marital woes. As I had that thought, I could feel a rumbling at the bottom of my stomach that moved quickly to my chest, My God, it's now in my throat! Before I could figure out what was happening, I threw up these words, "Girl! We have been having this same conversation for the past five years! We keep mulling over the same old s@#*! None of this is new! You have to **decide** what you want and move in that direction!" No sooner than the words left my lips, I began to experience something; a revelation or a new awareness that I had not experienced before. Though I said the words to her, almost as quickly as they spewed out of my mouth, the words seemed to rapidly and collectively morph into a visible, tangible being. It was as if I could see the entity walking in her direction. I began to recognize the "being" as a familiar silhouette—a curvy statuette that stood about five feet and three inches tall, with hips and shoulders neatly proportioned. As I looked on, it took a quick pause, then suddenly took a 180-degree turn and darted directly toward me. Startled by what I was seeing and feeling, these words stepped right in my face, slapped me on the forehead, and in my own voice spoke firmly, *Barbara, we've been having this same conversation for the past five years. We keep mulling over the same old stuff, talking about the same unfinished articles, the unfinished book, the business ideas, weight-loss, goals...your hopes...dreams. Why haven't you reached the goals you set for yourself? Why aren't you living the life you envisioned? None of this is new! You have to decide what you want and move in that direction!*

OMG! What just happened? Did I just have an out of body experience? I do not even remember ending the call with Len. The last thing I recalled was the silence I heard at the end of my diatribe. Len was completely quiet. In fact, we both were. She was likely trying to process what I said and had no clue what was happening to me on the other end. I could not verbalize the encounter I had with myself. I could only sit there in the heaviness of the silence cloaked around my neck.

In the dead of the quiet, I could hear the water swooshing about as the laundry tumbled through the wash cycle. At this point, it was difficult for me to tell if what I was hearing was real or not, but I was keenly conscious of it as it paralleled the swirling thoughts from the figurative slap on the forehead by this figurative "being" made up of words born from the rumbling in my stomach. It was if I was being lulled into a trance— *deeper...deeper...deeper.* This caused me a great deal of inner turbulence. I could no longer ignore the fact that I had not become who I wanted to be, accomplished the things that I had set out to accomplish, or even more sad for me—living the life that I wanted to live.

My rudders had been stuck for quite some time and I really did not know how to rescue myself and move forward. The words spoken, meant to push a friend into a different space, turned out to be just the jolt I needed to free myself from murky waters. I knew that if my life were finally going to go higher, I would have to go **DEEPER.**

So I *decided* I wanted my life to look different—a life that looked more like the one I had envisioned. To make that happen, I would have to get clear about what I wanted. It had been so long since I had even given my desires any consideration that, frankly, I had forgotten what I really wanted. So there, I sat, sending my mind out to wander. I took a deep breath, closed my eyes, and started making a mental list of what I wanted or goals that I had abandoned…

___*LOSE THE TEN POUNDS ALREADY!*

___*Save more money*

___*Declutter and get organized*

___*Find a system to get the laundry done, and keep it done*

___*Spend more time with my daughters*

___*Start writing again*

___*Help others more*

The list went on and on, but there were a couple things on it that stood out to me— "start writing again" and "help others more". These especially intrigued me because they were things that I absolutely found rewarding, but at some point had fallen from my list of priorities. It was time to hit the reset button and shift my focus to the things that were most important to me. Right there on the laundry room floor, I **DECIDED**! I decided that I was going to get back to doing what I had forgotten I wanted do! I declared it! I AM A WRITER who HELPS others live their best life!

Well, turns out that what I wanted was not the only thing that I had forgotten. I was in such a deep trance that I had forgotten that it was Christmas morning! I opened my eyes to the sound of my two little girls excitedly calling in search of me, "Mommy...Mommy! Where are you? He came...He came...Santa came to our house!" I snapped out of it and sprinted up the stairs. We all gathered around the tree and lined up the gifts in preparation for our gift giving tradition; but this time felt different. I could not help but notice that something inside of me had changed. I also could not help being distracted by the thoughts of my conversation with Len. I wondered if she was OK. If she had experienced a similar shift. Anxious, I gave into my temptation to check my phone to see if she had texted me. I grabbed it from the table and took a quick peek. My heart smiled when I read the message from her, "There's nothing like a swift kick from a good sister-friend to get you back on track. Thanks, for rescuing me from crazyland! I love you girl! Merry Christmas!"

Deeper Thinking:

It is likely that you have stumbled over one of the cracks in crazyland. It happened to me, it happened to Len, and I am quite certain that it happens to everybody at some point. At times, we all get stuck—feeling like our life just isn't what we envisioned it to be; not having a clue as to where to start. If you have lost your way or become a little foggy about what you really want, chances are, your life has left you a few clues. Take some time to contemplate what you want. You can start by making a list of things that make you happy, things that you want, goals, or tasks that you would like to complete. Now, do not overthink it. It can be something as simple as getting your closet organized or cleaning the kitchen; or a lifelong dream that needs that first step like getting that degree or writing a book. No matter how big or small, WRITE IT on the list! Journaling about what you want will help you get clear about your next steps.

Use the space below to record your thinking.

_____

_____

_____

_____

_____

_____

_____

_____

_____

_____

_____

What stands out to you on your list? Decide what you want and draw a picture of how it would look if you were in possession

Chapter

2

Examine *Your Life*

An unexamined life is not worth living.

~Plato

Now, **examining** my life proved more difficult than making the decision about what I wanted. It required courage to challenge my beliefs and look closely at patterns of behavior with a level of honesty that I had never engaged before. I asked myself, *Why? Why haven't I taken the actions necessary to acquire what I want, to live the life I want to live or to be who I had hoped to become?* If I were really going to move my life in the direction of my vision, I would have to face the answers that I could only find inside of me.

I had to get to the bottom of this; and at the bottom, is exactly where I thought I should start!

With birds singing and flowers in bloom, late March 2014 was the perfect time for this exploration. I literally went through the bottom of my desk drawer, found a folder labeled "personal" and started thumbing through it. I read a few writing pieces and found myself pleasantly surprised. I had to ask myself, *Girl, did you write this?* Before I knew it I had read at least six unfinished pieces; all beginnings of articles or books that I had planned to submit for publishing. In that same folder, I discovered a list of goals. One of them read, *I want to be a writer—a published author using my gift of writing to encourage others to be their best selves...finish article and submit for publication by November 3, 2007!* TWO THOUSAND SEVEN! Really!

SEVEN years had passed and still no published article, or completed for that matter!

Coming to grips with the time lapse, I angrily admonished myself, *Guess what Barbara, you want to be a writer, well, writers WRITE!* I was so disappointed and appalled at my progress. This paper trail clearly led to a graveyard of buried hopes and dreams that could only be excavated by a close examination of the *why* of my behavior. I just kept asking myself, *Why didn't I finish? Why the starting and stopping? Why haven't I finished anything— anything that would move me toward my vision anyway?*

After I got over the shock of my lack of productivity, I suited up in my figurative scuba gear and began the deep-sea dive rescue mission through my life. I swam past all kinds of creatures—excuses, busyness, procrastination, and the unwillingness to explore what I did not know. I maneuvered through the symbolic walls of seaweed and fungi and found the anchor that had held me locked in position for so long. I grabbed my net and fished out a recurrent pattern. Regardless of the goals I had set, year after year, I failed to accomplish what I wanted for myself. At the end of every year, I found myself dragging to a metaphoric shore a collection of unfinished projects or goals unattained.

When it came to my writing, I used the excuse of not having the right ambiance. As soon as I would sit down to write, I would notice that sock on the floor that just could not wait for me to pick it up. The sock drew my eye to the basket filled with the dirty clothes that were screaming to be washed. Then the mental banter would start, *I should probably light a candle and dim the lights; perhaps play some soft music. Oops! Now it is time to pick up the kids...or maybe I have time for a quick nap. Man, I really do not know where to start, how it should sound, or how to get this done at all. Never mind, I'll just figure it out tomorrow.* I was constantly, and often willingly, distracted by the little noises that life tends to create.

I recognized that my friend was stuck in a toxic relationship, and now I had discovered that I was in a similar cycle of toxicity; except the other person in this unhealthy relationship was me. I was fighting myself by sabotaging my progress and I had to figure out why. So I pulled up a chair and took a seat right at the edge of me. I became the quiet observer sent to examine my behavior.

I took a closer look at what I found on my deep dive—the unfinished writing pieces, the unrealized goals, the abandonment of who I was, and the excessive amount of time I squandered. I could actually flashback to the times that I convinced myself that I would get back to it tomorrow; only to have tomorrow come to find me distracted by cleaning the house, talking to friends, taking a nap, or anything to escape doing what I said I wanted to do. These were all unconscious avoidance tactics. As I scanned the writing samples and contemplated finishing, I could feel anxiety raising its persistent head. I took a cleansing breath and thought, *That's fear. You procrastinate. You make excuses. You tell yourself that you do your best work under pressure, but become overwhelmed and ultimately become paralyzed and get nothing done. You chalk it up as that's just who you are…but really, you have put this off because you have been afraid.* I realized that this pattern of delay and perpetual paralysis was born from a place of fear—fear that things could not actually happen for me, fear that my writing was not worth reading, fear…that it would be less than perfect.

There it was—the "P" word—perfectionism; submersed in the underbelly of procrastination. My obsession with the perception of others left me floundering to protect myself from their judgement; or maybe even my own. Instead of just writing for the love of writing or with the hope of inspiring others, I was writing in search of people's affirmation. Constantly worrying about what people would think or say kept my wheels spinning in the mud.

This behavior simply did not align with what I wanted for myself and had proven to be contrary to who I wanted to be. I could no longer live in this state of cognitive dissonance. This was just not who I was going to be anymore! After my deep dive examination, I decided that I was going to write as if I was only going to read it! I was going to finish even if I had to do it with my hands trembling and my heart pounding in my chest.

Deeper Thinking:

Procrastination, one of fear's best disguises, had become my anchor. It came dressed in busyness with other worthy activities—opportunities that distracted me from my original goals. It created a vicious cycle of inaction; a hamster wheel of frustration. You can have all of the goals you want, and have all of your affirmations memorized, but if you fail to identify the limiting patterns of your behavior, you will indeed become discouraged and quit. This is what happened to me time and time again.

I am curious, what have you stuffed in the bottom of the drawer; that thing you have always wanted to do, but can't seem to make it happen?

Use the space to journal what it would feel like to have it.

_____

_____

_____

_____

_____

_____

_____

_____

_____

_____

_____

So, what is holding you back? Are you getting in your own way? Examine the patterns of behavior that may be impeding your progress. Think about it and journal them here.

_____

_____

_____

_____

_____

_____

_____

_____

_____

_____

_____

_____

Chapter

3

Eliminate the Barriers

The only barriers that exist are those that we create and establish in our own minds.

~Napoleon Hill

Oprah Winfrey, the famous media mogul, tells of tumultuous times growing up, in rural Mississippi, a child of poverty, physical and emotional abuse, and having to break through the racial barriers of the television industry. Michael Jordan demonstrated his tenacity when he did not give up on his NBA dream after being cut from his high school basketball team; we can only imagine the mental leaps he had to take to jump over that wall; Jim Carry, prior to becoming a blockbuster movie star, was once homeless and with the vision of becoming an actor, wrote huge checks to himself to remind him to keep pushing. We have all heard the story of Bill Gates, the founder of Microsoft, dropping out of college and transforming the world of technology, of which we all are reaping the benefits. I am certain you would agree that these people had to eliminate barriers—climb over, run around, and bust through walls that stood between them and what they wanted to accomplish. But my encounter with Dr. Johnnetta McSwain left me speechless, tearful, and empowered all at the same time. I had never heard a story of overcoming, as painfully rewarding, as the one she shared at a conference I attended. The 48-year-old, award winning international speaker and author of *Rising Above the Scars*, captivated the audience of women as she told of her journey of breakdown and breakthrough.

I could feel the energy shift in the room as Dr. McSwain opened the session with delightful interactions with the audience. Her stage presence filled the room and we were completely engaged from the start. The mood would swing from glee to grief as she invited us to peek into her past. I just knew that I would have to include her story in my book to demonstrate that getting unstuck comes in all shapes and sizes. I was elated when she gave me her blessing to share parts of her life.

In the backwoods of Alabama, a 27-year-old Johnnetta ran smack dead into a wall as she found herself handcuffed in the back of a police car and consequently facing felony drug charges. "All I could think about was the fact that my son would have to be raised by my mother. I couldn't let that happen." Johnnetta described a pivotal moment in her life. I listened as she shared a heart-wrenching story of emotional, mental, and physical abuse. Born to an alcoholic mother and a father who abandoned her, she was raised in an environment in which the adults lacked the capacity to provide the guidance or be the refuge she so desperately needed. "I don't remember a time when my mother actually hugged me or told me that she loved me." She went on to describe how her mother's venomous verbal and physical attacks were riddled with putdowns that she would adopt as her own beliefs about herself. As an example, she told of a time when her mother told her that she would never amount to anything and she wished she were never born. "Please don't feel sorry for me! I don't tell my story for pity. I tell it to show people that you don't have to live a life dictated by your environment or by the choices of others. You get to choose…you get to **decide** what's included in your story. I speak and write to give you a picture of what breaking through looks like. I was constantly looking for something…someone outside of me to tell me I was good enough. This led me to do things that I shouldn't have done; even though I knew they were wrong. I had to change—my thoughts and my actions. I had to tell myself something different. Deep inside I knew I was better…that I could do better."

In the back of that police car, Johnnetta realized that she landed there because of the choices she made. As she sat with her hands cuffed behind her, she decided that she was going to create a different life for herself and her son; she was going to rewrite her story. As a first time offender, Johnnetta was sentenced to 1 year and 1 day in jail. She pleaded guilty and accepted a Felony charge with a 2-year probation. As soon as she was free, Johnnetta took all of the money she had, packed her clothes, left her Section 8 Housing, and drove to an apartment complex in Atlanta and started her new life. She was able to enroll in college, received a Bachelor's Degree in Communication from Kennesaw State University, a Master's Degree in Social Work from Clark Atlanta University, and went on to acquire a Doctoral Degree in Social Work, Policy and Administration. Now Dr. McSwain spends her time helping others eliminate barriers and break through walls erected by life's circumstances.

Johnnetta was determined to make the changes necessary to achieve a different outcome. Her very life depended on the radical steps that she would have to take to eliminate anything that would be a barrier to her success. She physically removed herself from the toxic culture in which she was so deeply enmeshed—moving 250 miles away. She got rid of all of the furniture in her little apartment in Alabama and threw away any items that would remind her of the life that she was leaving. She even had to eliminate some important relationships. Dr. McSwain's voice quivered as she closed, "One of the most difficult parts of my evolution was severing the ties with the poisonous people in my life. Strangely, I loved the very ones who were contributing to my demise. Some of them were dear friends, but most of them had a hand in raising me—they were my family."

Dr. McSwain's story is not my story. In fact, her family history is quite the antithesis of mine. However, we ran into some of the same walls. Growing up the youngest of 10 was like having my own little entourage to support and cheer me on from the very beginning. I remember times when my brothers and sisters would literally have physical fights over taking me, THE BABY, on a trip to a friend's house or showing me off to that someone special. My family openly celebrated my every milestone and constantly sent the "Midas Touch" message to me. When I started walking, they erupted with praises, "Yeah, the baby is walking!"; I said my first word, "Yeah, the baby is talking!" Every milestone: *the baby's going to school; the baby is graduating, the baby got her doctorate; the baby got a promotion,* was celebrated. Seeing Barbara "do" big things just became an unspoken norm. My family simply loves me. Though they were genuine in their doting, the constant admiration left me addicted to the approval of others; on an endless search for external affirmation and a closeted perfectionist. I found myself constantly needing people to affirm me; to tell me how well I did, how good I looked, or how much I inspired them to be better. I suffered from what I refer to as the pedestal syndrome—high on the pedestal is where people would automatically place me.

I did not solicit this position, gave no indication that I wanted to be there, and struggled to keep my balance atop such a narrow surface.

This need for the praise and approval of others and the need to have things just perfect established in me an overwhelming, negative belief. If no one was clapping, I felt that what I did or who I was just was not worthy of the stage. Though these were my private thoughts, this often showed up in my behavior—in my life choices.

I had become so dependent on the value that other people assigned to me that I did not recognize the trap being set for me as I fell head over hills in love with my husband. Early in the marriage to my college sweetheart, I was lavished with his praise and attention; he even pretended to be extremely supportive of me and my career. He was my biggest cheerleader as I would pursue the next degree or consider going for a promotion. I was so intoxicated with his adoration, that he was able to convince me that my goals were "our" goals.

The truth was, my husband's goal was to have me make more money so that he could fund his double life. My husband was having an affair. I learned this, as I have many of my life transforming lessons, through a deep, spiritual revelation and intuition. My husband came home from a "business trip". Came into the house, came upstairs, stuck his head in the guest room door, and greeted me as usual. Doing some work on the computer…as usual…I briefly acknowledged him and continued to work. He proceeded to the master where he quickly fell asleep. I went to sleep in the guest room; yep, this was the routine. A couple of hours later, I woke up in a panic! *I think I'm having a heart attack! My chest is so tight; I can barely breathe. What's wrong with me? Oh my God! Something's not right!* I was right, something was wrong, though it wasn't physical, my heart was definitely under attack.

I jump out of bed, grabbed the computer, got on the internet and started to check our cell phone bill. Somehow, I knew that I would find something. Trembling and feeling like I was about to die, I quickly scanned the bill and saw one particular number appear over and over again: early morning calls, calls in the middle of the day, but they usually stopped around 5:00 PM; the time he would get home from work. Just to confirm what I was thinking, I dialed the number and yep, a woman answered. I asked, "Do you know my husband?"; of course, she offered a denial. I knew as soon as I hung up, she was going to call him to warn him, so I ran into the master, flipped the light on and yelled, "Are you cheating on me?" His shoulders dropped, and seemingly relieved, he uttered, "I'm not happy."

What the hell! In the middle of me falling apart all by myself, now I've got to deal with this! Now I REALLY don't know who I am! Most of the "who" of me was connected to him, my husband. Who am I if I am not the love of my husband's life; if my husband has turned his back on me, turned his heart from me?

The pain and agony of realizing that the last twenty years of my life was an illusion of sorts, was bewildering. I was devastated. The man that my girls and I greeted at the door upon his return from his trips, was really returning to us from his other life—one in which we did not exist. Within thirty days of our divorce, he was engaged! *Who does that?* I was certain that this was a marriage made for a Lifetime Movie! I was furious! He did not just cheat on me. In their selfishness, he and his mistress cheated me out of my dream of family; they cheated my daughters of the stability of a traditional, cohesive family unit.

For a while after the discovery, I wallowed in my anger, disappointment, and disillusionment. The longer I sat in my puddle of self-pity, more and more people made my angry list. I blamed my family for cultivating an insatiable appetite for something, someone outside of myself to validate me. I blamed my friends who constantly looked for me to have it all together; and I blamed myself for meeting their expectations. I wanted to go to each of them and scream, *You were wrong! You taught me wrong! You treated me wrong! You ruined me*!

Unlike Dr. McSwain, I could not eliminate my family; I really did not want to. After all, they were well meaning and their praise and support came from a good place—a place of love. How could they know that their loving support would have an adverse effect? Contrarily, their love is what helped me to heal the gaping wounds of my failed marriage. My family was simultaneously everything that was wrong with me, and everything that was right. There were, however, some friends that I eliminated. I eliminated those that held high expectations for me, but not for themselves; those that were judgmental and secretly (so they thought) waited for me to fail. I eliminated the relationship with my former husband and many of his associates. Though I am flattered when people acknowledge my work, compliment me on my look, or even tell me how much I inspire them, I have eliminated the need for external affirmation.

The process of elimination illuminated some barriers that did not necessarily announce themselves as barriers. The actions of my family, friends, my husband—none were to blame for my paralysis.

Some of the things that I experienced were sad, unfortunate, and tragic even. Though these incidents were not my fault, it was certainly my responsibility to recreate the mosaic of my life. I had to take one hundred percent responsibility for where I was in my life, regain custody of myself, and well, forgive them, and more importantly forgive myself.

As I deactivated all of the negative magnetic forces in my life, I was able to break away from the negative thoughts that kept me in the cycle of procrastination. I made a conscious effort to practice replacing the thoughts and behaviors that landed me in crazyland. For every negative thought that would try to purchase real estate in my mind, I would outbid it with a counter-thought. Any time that I would begin to doubt myself, that negative mental chatter would begin—*Are they going to like this? I don't know if they'll get it.* I would combat it with, *Barbara, there are a lot of best sellers that you have read that* you *did not like, but that did not change the fact that a lot of other people loved it! The point is that not everybody is going to like what you write or even support everything that you do, but that does not negate its quality or diminish its worth...or yours. Not every person prefers the BMW®, uses an iPhone®, or eats meat, but an extraordinary amount of these products are sold around the world every single day!* I continue to use this practice often. Every time the negative mental chatter rears its ugly head, I punch it with a counter-thought. Changing my thinking and learning to shift my perspective have been key to eliminating the barriers and staying unstuck.

My answer to procrastination was to stay focused on what I wanted. Whenever I would feel that urge to put it off another day, I would take out my journal and read the statement that I had written describing what I wanted "to help people through my writing". This practice reminded me of my earlier declaration—I AM A WRITER WHO INSPIRES PEOPLE TO LIVE THEIR BEST LIVES! Well, WRITERS WRITE! Now, I give myself a 10-second count down and spring into action. I do not over think it, over analyze it, think about the judgement of other people, how it sounds, or what it looks like in print. I just write!

Now that I was clear about what I wanted and confident in who I am, the need for approval, external affirmation, and the unreasonable reach for perfection dissipated. The notion that I could not produce writing worthy of my readers' approval or match the level of quality to which I had become accustomed had been debunked. At this point, it was only logical that I could achieve the goals connected to my secret dreams.   This revelation caused a revolution in my thinking...in my life!   Just what I needed to *eliminate* the behaviors that pinned me down.   Like Dr. McSwain, I had to start telling myself a different story.

Deeper Thinking:

Many of us could likely share a story of living up to the expectations of others—constantly seeking external affirmation and outside sources of validation. Perhaps we could all share a story of overcoming of some sort; a story of living a life based on what other people think. Often the barriers that we encounter are the result of beliefs firmly established as a part of our thought process long before we developed the ability to think for ourselves. We adopt belief systems of our family members, friends, spouses, school, church, and society; taking on the personas, beliefs, and truths that others create in us. As I traced the origin of my barriers, I was able to strike down those things that were not true, crush the six-foot

wall brick by brick and jump over the pile. I
am confident that you can do the same.

When a barrier is revealed by negative thoughts, what is the first feeling that surfaces for you? Where do you feel it in your body? Can you remember the first time you felt this way?

_____

_____

_____

_____

_____

_____

_____

_____

_____

_____

_____

_____

_____

_____

_____

What limiting beliefs have become barriers to your success? Where did those come from? What negative thoughts do you have about what you would like to achieve or the life that you want to create?

_____

_____

_____

_____

_____

_____

_____

_____

_____

_____

_____

_____

_____

_____

What successes can you identify in your life that required you to overcome barriers and eliminate any negative myths that have played out in your behavior?

_____

_____

_____

_____

_____

_____

_____

_____

_____

_____

_____

_____

_____

_____

_____

_____

Chapter

4

Plan *of Action*

Inaction breeds doubt and fear. Action breeds confidence and courage.

~Dale Carnegie

I AM A WRITER WHO INSPIRES PEOPLE TO LIVE THEIR BEST LIVES! Well, WRITERS WRITE!

There! I had **D**ECIDED that I was going to write. I dug deep, took the necessary steps, and truthfully **E**XAMINED my life; this helped me to recognize the pattern of behaviors that impeded my progress. Once I could name the barriers that stood between my success and me, I ELIMINATED them. Now, it was time to make it happen—time to activate a PLAN OF ACTION!

Well, nothing just happens! You do not just wake up in the morning at a certain time, brush your teeth, take a shower, wash your face, get dressed, jump in your car, drive to Starbucks® and pick up your coffee, and end up at work. Though parts of this routine may be accomplished unconsciously, at some point you established a *plan of action.* You decided that you would wake up at a specific time and set the alarm for that time. You planned. You decided that you did not want to offend people with your stinky breath, so you planned to brush your teeth. You decided to take a shower and you sprang into action and jumped right in. You felt it was necessary to be fully awake and present so you planned and allotted enough time to stop and get your cup of Joe on your way in to the office! You were able to accomplish a comprehensive morning routine and get to work on time all because you planned and took the necessary actions to ensure your success.

As haphazard as your morning routine may seem, it falls into a simple plan of action that at some point became institutionalized in your life. You decided what you wanted to accomplish and you created the conditions and took the appropriate actions to achieve the desired outcome. On some level, you knew that nothing, really just happens without specific steps and supportive actions—without intentionality, nothing just happens.

No matter how many bold, well-intended goals you have established for yourself, you will become increasingly frustrated and waver in your confidence to achieve them if you do not establish a clear plan of action. This is true for you, and became profoundly revelatory for me as I began this journey.

In a period of six months, I got a divorce, accepted a career reassignment from one leadership position to another, purchased a house, sold a house, sent a child off to college, and started a life and leadership coaching business to help women (like me) in leadership transition through life changing events. All of this in the middle of experiencing the roller coaster ride of my own healing process, and fastening the seat belts of my two daughters as they navigated their new reality. So, I asked myself, *Just how in the hell was I supposed to fit this writing thing in?*

I had a little squirrel in my personality and at times found it difficult to maintain my focus on a given project for an extended period. Yep! I was a squirrel.

No longer obsessed with what people thought about me, I now had to manage me; those little quirks in my personality that could derail me. I knew that I had a book in me—my entire life had prepared me for it and I was determined to get it done! By nature, I am a visionary, a conceptual thinker. I see things as they should, would, or could be. I think in finished product. This often worked well in my role as a leader in my career; being able to cast a compelling vision and assemble teams to make the dream a reality are essential to success. The problem here was that this was not a professional goal of mine and there were not people on the payroll waiting for me to lead them. This was a personal goal and I was the team. I was responsible for casting the vision and making my dreams come true. Yes, I was determined, but I had a little bit of pee running down my leg. I was scared. I did not want to get stuck in the dream or go running back to crazyland, but I did not quite know how to handle the details. Frankly, the details only frustrated me (I guess that is why they say it is where the devil lives). I knew that if I did not see the manifestation of my vision quickly, I would retreat to Dreamland, get more ideas that would likely distract me, come up with new projects, or change the direction with this one. I had a tendency to dream big, start with a grand opening, spike for about 90 days, and fall flat of meeting my ultimate goals. Over the years, I have come to know this about myself and learned the importance of being intentional and strategic in planning to reach my goals.

I did not quite trust myself to get this done on my own. I needed a support system. I put my leadership skills to work and I put together my team. I began seeing a therapist to help me manage my emotions and support my girls. I hired a realtor who was responsible for the sale of the marital property and getting me into my new home; learned the value of FaceTime to keep the lines of communication open with my daughter who was a college freshman; hired a mentor to help me with my new business; and got myself a writing coach.

I had to learn how to manage it all and I knew that I could not do this alone, so I solicited the help of my squad.

To fulfill my dream of encouraging others through writing, I also had to create the time and space in my life to breathe, think, and actually write.

I literally cleared an area in my home and claimed it as "MINE"…and marked it as such. I committed to completing just one of the unfinished writing samples that I found in the bottom of the desk drawer. I thought this goal was narrow enough to obtain in a short period (quick wins help with motivation). I bought a special journal specifically for this process. In it, I included a weekly schedule of days and times that I would dedicate to writing, a section for goal setting, and a place to record weekly assessments of my progress. My writing coach provided guidance and helped me to grow and develop as a writer. During our weekly meetings, she would assign homework that we would review each session. This helped me to stay focused on specific tasks between meetings and kept me moving forward; knowing that she was going to hold me accountable kept inaction, excuses, and procrastination at bay.

Perhaps as you read this you may be thinking, *I can't afford to hire all of those people...or who could not reach their goals with all those resources?* Well, that is what my secretary said to me in so many words. She is extremely creative, talented, and passionate about gift wrapping. When she is wrapping a gift for someone, she thinks of every detail. If she knows the person, she considers their personality, the occasion, and what the gift would mean to them.

"It's more than just giving someone a gift." She told me in a tone that protected her craft. Mrs. Waller is in her 50's. She stands about six feet tall, and has a head full of silver hair cut into a funky, sassy style; her eyes are so big and bright and eyelashes so pronounced that she makes me think of the cartoon character, Betty Boop. Without saying a word, it is clear that she is in the room. In all of her grander, she sashayed into my office and presented me with a sample of a gift that I could present to my staff upon their return from summer vacation. I was stunned at the thought and level of detail she had put into just wrapping the gift. For the men, she had the wrapping in the shape of striped neckties on a collared shirt. For the women, she had the boxes look like dresses adorned with the perfect accessories, and...get this...shoes. The dresses had the shoes to match! I was flabbergasted.

After I hooted and hollered in awe of the gift wrapped boxes, I burst out, "Don't you know people would pay you to do this?" She got quiet, sat down, tempered my excitement and began to express her frustration. She shared that her husband and 18 year old daughter had been ill; both dealing with serious health issues. Two years prior, her husband was diagnosed with heart disease; shortly after his diagnosis, her daughter was diagnosed with juvenile diabetes. "I just don't have time!" Mrs. Waller bellowed. I knew this sense of helplessness all too well. She was under a great deal of pressure to manage it all, but the one thing that she was not managing was herself. As women, we do this often.

Mrs. Waller went on to explain that the time it takes to make sure her daughter has the food she needs and is assured that her husband was taking his medicine, left very little time for her to take care of herself—to work toward her dream. I get it. We all have life going on in the middle of our lives. I am not insensitive or oblivious to the fact that people are experiencing "real" issues, but the consequences of not attending to your own needs could be far more devastating. Life will certainly throw us curve balls, but we have to become more facile at changing the position of the glove so that we are still able to catch the ball; or, just be ok with not catching it at all. In other words, there are always solutions to the challenges we face. Many times, the solution may be found in our perspectives.

As Mrs. Waller lamented, I kindly (well, maybe not so kindly) interrupted, "So, you have to **D**ECIDE. What is it that you really want? Mrs. Waller answered, "I really want to start a gift wrapping business but, again, I just don't have the time or the money and I don't really know where to start!" Mrs. Waller was a nurturer by nature.

During the months of us working together, I had become familiar with her family history. She was born the eldest child to an adolescent mother and was often thrusted into the role of caretaker for her younger siblings. In reflective **EXAMINATION**, I pointed out the pattern to her. She had become this super-responsible wife and mother who felt like the earth would implode if she was not there to inflate it with her very own breath.

I pressed her a bit and proceeded with a list of questions: *What can you **E**LIMINATE?* "Your daughter is 18 now, can you and the doctor work with her to teach her how to choose her own foods?" I asked. "You have older children, can they help you with taking care of your husband...their dad? What else can you take off of your plate?" I also asked, "What steps have you taken already? Have you written down what you would like to do? How would you feel to have what you want? Who would you like to do it for or with? How much time can you set aside each week to think about what you want or to work toward your goals? Have you researched companies or searched the web to see if there are some local gift-wrapping businesses that you can visit to get ideas?"

My list of questions went on. I wanted to help her to open her eyes to the possibilities if she just organized a **P**LAN OF ACTION.

Not long after our conversation, Mrs. Waller came in with a little notebook dedicated to her dream of opening her gift-wrapping business. She shared her goals and was ecstatic about what she learned through her research. She even reached out to a couple of stores and asked if she could display some of her gift wrapped boxes. I was so thrilled to be a witness to her progress. When she truly *d*ecided what she wanted, *e*xamined her life, *e*liminated the behaviors that were holding her back, she was able to put together her *p*lan of action and started working her plan. She started doing demonstrations for women's groups and doing some gift-wrapping at their requests. She began working more and more.

The last I spoke to her, she had landed a gift wrapping gig with a couple of major department stores! The management of the local stores allow her to come into the store on weekends and set up a gift-wrapping booth. Her progress has been astounding!

The **P**lan of Action phase, not only acts as an accountability system of sorts, but it keeps you excited about your goals. As you begin to see things unfold in your favor, you just want to stay in actions. Having a clear plan literally assists in moving your life in the desired direction.

Mrs. Waller took a different approach. There was no cost associated with her action plan—carving out time to plan; to actually do the footwork involved in doing the research, visiting stores, and making the phone calls. It really did not cost her anything to borrow a few minutes of the business owners' or store managers' time to share her vision or to glean from their stories of stardom. She needed people, but she did not need them in the same what that I did. Everyone's needs are different; which means that your approach might be different, the steps you take might look different, but the results—reaching your goals—will be the same!

Come on! You can do this people!

Deeper Thinking:

Once I decided what I wanted for myself, tunneled through all of the roots, and cut away the kudzu, I was ready for ACTION! This worked for Mrs. Waller as well. She had decided what she wanted and was ready to go after it.

So, what do you want? Go back to your **"Deeper Thinking"** journal section in Chapter 1. What did you DECIDE that you wanted?

_____

_____

_____

_____

_____

_____

_____

_____

Do you still want the same thing…in the same way that you wanted it, or has your idea or desire for it changed?

Record your thoughts here:

_____

_____

_____

_____

_____

_____

_____

_____

_____

_____

_____

_____

_____

_____

_____

Based on what you want, establish a goal that you would like to accomplish. Be specific.

Example: I wanted to write a book, but establishing a smaller goal of writing at least one article by a specified date, made the goal more tangible and realistic for me. Mrs. Waller's goal was to start a thriving gift-wrapping business, but she started displaying gift boxes in stores and doing demonstrations for small groups. Be realistic in your goal setting. Set yourself up for quick wins!

_____

_____

_____

_____

_____

_____

_____

_____

What action steps will you take to ensure your success?

_____

_____

_____

_____

_____

_____

_____

_____

_____

_____

_____

_____

_____

_____

_____

_____

_____

Chapter

5

Evaluate *Your Progress*

Be strategic in your practices and watch yourself progress.

- Dr. Barbara Swinney

You have done the work! You decided, examined, eliminated, established a plan of action, and now...In my Dr. Phil's voice, *How's that working for you?* If I was going to create the conditions for perpetual success, I had to adopt a system that would answer that question. I needed a systematic way to **evaluate** my progress along the way. As I worked to find the most effective way to monitor and adjust my action steps, I began to examine some of my current practices in my role as leader and life coach. There were certain processes that I used unconsciously and I thought starting there would give me a clue as to how to evaluate and monitor my personal progress. I needed something simple; easy to use and readily applicable. I started paying close attention to how I did everything; from cleaning my house, processes that I would follow at work, and practices that I would use to get results with my coaching clients.

As an elementary school principal, I was charged with evaluating the job performance of teachers. However, I preferred to operate more like a coach instead of the "dreaded" evaluator. I thought about a time when I worked with one of my teachers to become more effective in the use of instructional practices.

With a casual walk through his fourth grade classroom, I stopped at a few students' desks and asked them what they were learning. None of them could clearly articulate what they were supposed to learn or why they were being asked to do the work they were doing. HOUSTON!...We have a problem! *If students were not clear about what they are supposed to know, or be able to execute the lesson as a result of the teacher's instruction, how were they going to become skilled in the application of new knowledge; if they could not even tell me what they were learning and why? YIKES!*

Before leaving the class, I wrote a note to the teacher, Mr. James, and left it on his desk: "Please stop by office after dismissal."

In hindsight, it probably was not a good idea—a bit insensitive even—to leave a note like that on a teacher's desk with no explanation. No matter how old you are, or what position you hold, no one wants to be called to the principal's office!

As soon as the last bell rang for dismissal, Mr. James came to my office. I heard a timid knock on the opened door. I looked up to Mr. James', usually pink complexion, completely washed white! Clearly, he was having some trepidation about coming to speak to me. I learned that no matter how genuine my intentions were or how desperately I wanted to help by coaching him to improvement, he only looked at me as his evaluator, ready to pounce; just waiting to judge him. It is the phenomenon of fear of the opinion of the outside observer that we all, at some point, experience.

I welcomed Mr. James into my office. I opened the conversation with a few pleasantries to put him at ease and then began with some probing questions: What were you expecting to come from the lesson you taught today? How do you usually convey the desired goal to students? How do you know if they have learned what you have taught? I did not want to simply describe my experience with his students. I wanted to raise his level of awareness so that he could come to some of his own conclusions while I supported him through the questioning. He admitted that he was curious about my interactions with his students while I was in his room and confessed that he just had to ask them what I had spoken to them about. By the time he finished speaking to his students, it had become clear to him that they were not able to effectively articulate their learning. Mr. James took a deep breath and became more tense. He slid down in his chair a tad; a little afraid of how I would respond. Visibly frustrated, he blurted, "It seems my students are not learning what I'm teaching or they just don't seem to understand what they're doing when they're working independently."

Yes! He got it! His awareness of the problem kicked the door of opportunity wide open! You cannot effectively address an issue if you do not even realize that there is actually an issue to address.

As a way to support him in improving the instructional delivery in his classroom, he and I collaborated to establish an improvement plan. He identified one goal: ensure that students were able to clearly articulate their learning. He wanted to focus and outlined specific action steps that he would take to achieve his goals. Over a period of six weeks, I observed Mr. James, spoke to his students, and met with him weekly to provide feedback and coach him in adjusting his classroom practices. Every week we would begin our session with his goal, discuss actions steps taken; modify, eliminate, or add strategies that he would implement in his classroom, and then plan for the following week. The weekly evaluation of his progress allowed him to achieve the goal he noted in the plan. As he and I examined the plan together, marked improvement was clear to both of us. He *decided* what he wanted, began to work intentionally toward his goals, and soon began seeing results.

At the close of our final meeting, I noticed that Mr. James' complexion had return to its normal pinkish hue; he was beaming with pride and excited about his new path to continuous success. I asked him to what he attributed his success. He paused briefly as if to ponder. "What a difference it makes to have a specific plan and structure in place. Evaluating my actions each week held me accountable and helped me to make the adjustments necessary for improvement. Without this process, I don't think I would have ever been able to make this type of progress," Mr. James graciously explained.

The evaluation process used with Mr. James, is the same process that I had used with many other teachers, as well as with my coaching clients. It was a process that I had internalized and often used without thinking much about it. As I reflected intently on the steps, a specific pattern emerged. When Mr. James and I would sit down each week, we would REVIEW the identified goal, REVISIT and REFLECT on the action steps, REVISE the plan as needed, and REPEAT the process with regularity. I now refer to it as my 5R Good® Strategy.

I realized that this method's application could be generalized to evaluate progress toward any goal, including progress toward my goal of become a writer. I had to become the teacher; and now, I was my own client!

Throughout my D-E-E-P-E-R journey, I was able to identify quite a few parallels between the strategies used for my business, organizational, and professional successes with those that I wanted to experience in my personal life. Particularly, establishing a systematic way to **EVALUATE** my progress.

I had *decided* that I wanted to write to inspire others. What did that look like in practical terms? Ultimately, I wanted to produce a book, but given my pattern of starting and stopping and my inexperience in writing for a real audience, I wanted to narrow my goal a bit to build my confidence as a writer and ensure my success—setting myself up for a win. So instead of setting my eye on the prize of a book, my goal was simply to complete one of the many articles that I started and get it published. This is the goal I wrote verbatim: Complete one article by February 26 and submit it to magazines by March 26.

With that goal plastered boldly on chart paper on the wall of my writing area, I *reviewed* it weekly. This was an important step because it ensured that I was on target with my action steps; all action steps needed to lead me to this very specific goal. Then, I would take the time to *revisit* my action steps; *reflecting* on what I had actually planned to do to meet my goal, assess whether the actions were done effectively and then *revise* the steps if necessary. *Repeating* this process each week helped me to take an objective look at my progress. I treated myself in the same way that I would treat a coaching client.

Another quick strategy that I would use is what I like to call my "WOW!®" Strategy. This strategy helped me to dig a little deeper into the details of my plan. Each week I created my "WOW! ®" List. I made a list of all of the tasks associated with my goals that I could accomplish **W**ithin **O**ne **W**eek. At the end of each week, I pulled out my list and **evaluated** my progress. For example, one of my strategies was to write for at least thirty minutes a day, three days out of the week. If I saw that I only wrote one day during that week, I would do a quick **examination** to find out why. If I got to the bottom of why and found procrastination, again, I would dig **DEEPER** until I got to the bottom of the procrastination, **eliminate** it by pulling it up at the root and was sure to establish the conditions **(plan of action)** necessary to overcome the issue. On the other hand, if I find that I indeed met my goal of writing thirty minutes a day, three days that week, I celebrated my progress, set new goals for the next week, and continued to move forward.

Some weeks I was extremely proud of myself for going above and beyond the goals I set. I would note, "You ROCK!" as a means of celebrating my progress. On others, I did not do squat…jack…donuts…NOTHING! Life happens! Do not judge me. I was very careful not to be overly critical of myself if I did not get everything checked off the list. I would simply make the adjustment the following week and keep it moving, honey! I did, however, quickly assess "why" before moving on. I wanted to make sure that I did not begin repeating any old behavior that could send me back into paralysis.

Unlike so many other times in my history, I actually finished the article by February 26, submitted to a magazine by March 26! And guess what? I was published!

****

The weekly **evaluations** of my goals and actions really worked to keep me on target. No matter what I found when I looked back, I was always pleased because I knew exactly what I needed to do to regroup and reengage in the process.

Mr. James' goal was to improve his instructional deliver. My goal was to write to inspire, but no matter what your goal is, an intentional evaluation process is essential. Not only in your goal setting, but in your supportive actions and strategies as well. You have to develop a systematic way of **evaluating** your progress.

If your goal is to lose weight, your goal could read like this: I will lose 10 pounds by date or…in 45 days. You want to make sure you keep this goal somewhere visible or readily accessible so that you are able to review it each week. Revisit your action steps. Did you actually workout and eat a proper diet? Reflect on what worked or what did not work. Revise your plan of action if necessary and repeat the process over and over again until you reach your goal.

If you find that you, indeed, met your weight loss target…Celebrate! Run around the kitchen naked!

During your weekly **evaluations**, you might find that you did not meet your weight loss target. Quickly **examine** your strategies to make sure you adhered to your **plan of action.** Identify and

eliminate any behavior that may have impeded your progress, and then regroup and reengage the process.

Deeper Thinking:

Throughout this process, I relied heavily on some of the **evaluation** strategies that I used in my role as a leader of an organization and a life coach. Well, get this: you are your own organization—YOU.org. You are a corporation, company, or entity that employs people to produce results or products. The only difference is that you represent the organization in its entirety; you are the organization *and* the client or customer. *You* are it. If it is your organization's mission is to provide effective services or products, how will you know when you have reached your goals or met your quotas? How will you know how well you are doing or what adjustments you need to make? You will not, unless you have a system, by which you **EVALUATE** your progress.

Take some time right now to evaluate your
progress. What goals have you established
for yourself? Did you create the conditions
to reach your goals? Did you allow enough
time for this goal?

_____

_____

_____

_____

_____

_____

_____

_____

_____

_____

_____

_____

_____

_____

What supportive strategies or action steps have you put in place to ensure that you reach your goals?

_____

_____

_____

_____

_____

_____

_____

_____

_____

_____

_____

_____

_____

_____

What is working? What is not working?

_____

_____

_____

_____

_____

_____

_____

_____

_____

_____

_____

_____

_____

_____

_____

_____

How can you improve? What adjustments do
you need to make?

_____

_____

_____

_____

_____

_____

_____

_____

_____

_____

_____

_____

_____

_____

_____

_____

What do you need to celebrate?

_____

_____

_____

_____

_____

_____

_____

_____

_____

_____

_____

_____

_____

_____

_____

_____

_____

Remember to spend some time reviewing your successes. It is important that you remind yourself that you have had many more successes than failures.

Chapter

6

Realize *That You Can Do It!*

Father, please remove all of the "I can't do it's from my body.

~Jhardé Swinney, age 8

The Christmas morning text from a friend turned out to be the best gift ever—truly, the gift that keeps on giving. That day, I began a life long journey of moving my life forward. I began going DEEPER in every area of my life; especially when I realized that I was stalled. Whether it was improving productivity at work, cleaning the closet or the junk drawer, or seeing my most personal dreams come true, I had discovered a strategy that worked! Going DEEPER has helped me to **realize** *that I can do it!*

Writing this book was a big deal for me. Not for the reasons that you may think. You see, I knew that I could write—though my writing was generally to serve the purpose of academia, using words in a way that clearly communicated a message to people always came easy to me. From college papers, memos to staff, or speeches for graduation, the mechanics of writing were often a breeze. I completely enjoyed the process, as long as my writing did not have a thing to do with me! As long as it did not require me to reveal anything beneath my milk chocolate skin or allow you to take a deeper look into these big brown eyes. I was not going to allow anyone to cross the boarders of my perfectly constructed fortress. You could paddle in your little boat in the moat that surrounded my stacked stone castle, but I would not dare let down the bridge or open the gates, invite you past the walls and let you trample on my pristinely manicured lawn. I had worked too hard to build this!

The moment I decided that I was going to put a book out into the world, I knew I would have to risk you seeing my imperfections—seeing that my lawn is not always trimmed and the doors on the castle sometimes squeaks or literally fall off the hinges! But it was time. Time for me to get over myself. I expended a great deal of mental energy on this book; it was time to make something different happen.

The actual writing process, I learned, had far more to do with just getting the words on the page; more than stringing thoughts together so that they make sense to the reader and ending up with a literal book in my hand. This project was about me getting out of my own way!

About every other week, Toni, my writing coach, and I were knocking out about one chapter, solving one problem after another, or accomplishing something with this book, until we got to Chapter 3. I got stuck on Chapter 3, Eliminating the Barriers. How ironic! Right in the middle of this book, I was stuck on the chapter that was supposed to help you get unstuck. It is hilarious now, but at the time, I wanted to have Toni meet me some place so that I could do a karate chop in the back of her head. She kept pushing me to go deeper. I kept going right up to the edge of the ocean, allowing the waves to sweep the water over my feet, but too afraid to jump right in! Toni, stood there behind me waiting for the right time to push me in. She knew that I was being protective of myself; cautious of who may be caught in the crossfire of my story. Toni was the fear whisperer—she could sense it as she read my writing. She was not quite sure what I was hiding, but she could just tell, that the "all out writer" that wrote Chapters 1 and 2, was suddenly not going all out; not sharing everything that she knew was inside of her. It took me much longer than our usual turnaround time to finish Chapter 3. I could feel self-doubt begin to kick in. I started thinking; *maybe*

I can't do this, maybe I'm not a writer, maybe, this was just another one of my big thinker dreams.

During one of our sessions, Toni got honest with me. In her stern, mama voice she coaxed, "Listen, Barbara, nobody is going to read this but me. Just write as if no one is ever going to read it...make it one of your journal entries. Just get it out there. If you don't like it, we can change it during the editing process. Let them in. You said you wanted to write this book to help other people, let the people in."

That night, I opened my heart, took to Chapter 3 and let it rip! So what if people knew what was happening in my life. After all, is this not the point of living—sharing your experiences so that someone else can see that they are not alone. Hearing my story and learning about my personal challenges could actually help other people deal with their own.

So I did it! I shared my story. The experiences that cultivated this new me. I have to tell you, getting it all out was so liberating. I was no longer a prisoner in my own castle; no longer stuck behind the walls of the fortress I had erected. I was free to take my shoes off and run through the grass, prop the doors open, and enjoy the conversations that you and I would have on my pristinely manicured lawn!

I finally got it all on paper and hit send. Toni's response to my submission: "You did it! I knew you could."

Not only have I realized that I can do it, I have also come to realize that I could always do it. I felt like Dorothy in the Wizard of Oz, "Just click your heels three times...you've always had the power!"

I sincerely believe that we all come to this earth with the ability to do, be, or have anything that we want; as long as these things are aligned with good. We are born knowing that we can.

Three-year-old Henry reminded me of this recently. On a visit to my house with his father and his 10-year-old brother Victor, Henry was a little timid initially. He quietly walked around my place as if he was scoping it out. I am sure he was contemplating what was in it for him. After just a few minutes, Henry spotted a box of cereal on the countertop. As if he had discovered something new, he belted out, "Cereal, I want cereal!" None of us paid much attention at first. So Henry decided that he would come up with a different plan of action. He walked up to the counter and pulled down the opened box of cereal. Just before Henry could make a huge mess, Victor leaped into action and scolded, "No, no, no, Henry!" By this time, I walked into the room and saw what was happening. Henry persisted. He had decided what he wanted and was determined that, by any means necessary; he was going to get it. "Cereal, you want cereal, Henry?" I asked. I took the box of cereal, asked him if he preferred dry cereal or if he wanted milk, and poured him a bowl. Henry climb up to the table and ate his cereal as if no one was in the room. He was so focused on what he wanted and enjoying his accomplishment until we simply disappeared.

Henry decided what he wanted and realized that with the right resources, he could actually have what he wanted. He put his plan into action and his little world responded.

Henry took me back a bit. He reminded me that we start our lives with such clarity and confidence. As toddlers, we saw the toy, decided right away that it was what we wanted, and then did not think twice about whether or not we could have it. We just had it in us to go and get it! We did not care what barriers we had to break through, climb over, or go around to get it. We simply went after it because in a toddler's mind, there is just nothing that you want that you cannot have. However, big people, like Victor, that the toddler has grown to love and trust, often unconsciously, begin to set limitations; teaching us what we can and cannot do.

We begin to internalize the "NO, NO, NO's" that lead to the maybe I can't.

Well, it is time for us to return to toddlerhood! Close our ears to the "No, No, No's" and focus like Henry! Go DEEPER and tap into your inner toddler! Go after that thing you have been wanting. Live the life that you want to live. You already have everything you need to get what you want; it is in you! It is time that you **REALIZE THAT YOU CAN DO IT**!

Deeper Thinking:

I became a little annoyed with my friend that Christmas morning, but the truth is, I do not think you would be reading this book had I not responded to her S.O.S. text. I do not even think I would have realized that I was stuck. It is likely that I would be in the same old space, in the same state of suppression, and living the same old life. It is easy to slip into the abyss and forget how big we are, how powerful we are, how absolutely, capable we are. I am thankful for all of the little reminders that were sent to me along the way. Dr. McSwain, Mr. James, Mrs. Waller, Toni, and Henry all became integral parts of my DEEPER journey. Though they may never know the magnitude of the role they each played, my life is forever transformed as they all helped me *realize* that I can indeed, do it!

Reflect on the DEEPER experiences you have had throughout the book. What have you come to *realize* about your capacity to get what you want?

_____

_____

_____

_____

_____

_____

_____

_____

_____

_____

_____

_____

How does it feel to have this new awareness?

_____

_____

_____

_____

_____

_____

_____

_____

_____

_____

_____

_____

_____

_____

_____

_____

What will you now accomplish as a result?

_____

_____

_____

_____

_____

_____

_____

_____

_____

_____

_____

_____

_____

_____

_____

_____

It's
Always
DEEPER

Epilogue

Living the DEEPER Life®

Living the DEEPER Life®

If you want your life to go higher, you have to go DEEPER!

Going DEEPER is not a one and done strategy or a disposable tool you use and toss. Instead, DEEPER is a lifestyle; a way of living. It is a way to achieve perpetual success in every area of your life. To maintain a forward moving lifestyle, continue to apply the principles to your life. Be intentional in your application and you are certain to notice the interconnectedness of the practices. You will become more facile in achieving your goals; finding yourself living the life you want to live. Continue your DEEPER journey. I present the review of these steps to you as a gift that keeps on giving. It's time that you...

Decide - Clarify your vision and get clear about what you would like to accomplish. Deciding what you want is the first and most important step in living the DEEPER Life. Once you are clear about what you want, you will find that actually getting what you want will become easier. Consciously or unconsciously, we are making decisions about the direction of our lives daily. Jump into the driver's seat and take control of where you are going; accomplish your goals, big or small, and begin living the life you want to live. Decide what you want, align your behaviors, and watch how you move from where you are to where you want to be!

Examine - Identify behaviors that have impeded your progress and consciously examine your life. Figure out why you do what you do. Reflect on your life in an effort to discover patterns of behaviors prompted by a belief system established in you before you were conscious of your thinking or thought processes. As you walk through your life, you will find similarities in the behaviors that occur during different periods when you felt stuck. Examining your life will help you climb over the walls that have entrapped you.

Eliminate - Replace negative behaviors or thoughts with those that move you toward your goals. Eliminate the barriers to creating the life that you want as the origin of patterns are revealed and debunked. This is where you get over the hump of paralysis and overcome some of my own limiting beliefs.

Plan - Determine the steps necessary to get what you want! Be specific and intentional as you plan. By establishing a Plan of Action you will create paths that will allow you to realize your goals. The Plan of Action phase acts as an accountability system and keeps you excited about your goals. As you begin to see things unfold in your favor, you will want to stay in action. Having a clear plan literally assists in moving your life in the desired direction, over and over again!

Begin operating on purpose and realize your dreams through a strategic, intentional process that keeps you in action.

Evaluate - Get honest with yourself regarding your progress. Celebrate and make adjustments as necessary. Determine a systematic way to **E**valuate Your Progress. You may certainly adapt the processes that we talked about in Chapter 5, or you may already know of a system; just find the evaluation process that works for you. Reflecting on what is working and understanding the necessary changes you need to make will help you produce your desired results.

Realize *That You Can Do It!* - Apply these principles and you WILL reach your goals and become who you want to be! As you adopt the DEEPER Lifestyle, you'll realize that you can indeed have the things that you want, reach your goals, and live the live that you want to live. Go back through the chapters in this book and take a DEEPER look. In your new level of awareness, you will see some things that you did not recognize before and come to new realizations. Begin recording what is happening in your life as you begin living the DEEPER Lifestyle!

My

DEEPER

Thinking

Journal

My DEEPER Thinking Journal

_____

_____

_____

_____

_____

_____

_____

_____

_____

_____

_____

_____

_____

When your vision is clear, making decision

become easy.

~Walt Disney

My DEEPER Thinking Journal

_____

_____

_____

_____

_____

_____

_____

_____

_____

_____

_____

_____

The only limitations that you have are the ones that you've created and established in your own mind.

~Nepoleon Hill

My DEEPER Thinking Journal

_____

_____

_____

_____

_____

_____

_____

_____

_____

_____

_____

_____

_____

_____

_____

Your life is waiting for you to show up!

~Dr. Barbara L. Swinney

My DEEPER Thinking Journal

_____

_____

_____

_____

_____

_____

_____

_____

_____

_____

_____

_____

_____

Deciding what you want compels you to take action!

~Dr. Barbara L. Swinney

My DEEPER Thinking Journal

_____

_____

_____

_____

_____

_____

_____

_____

_____

_____

_____

_____

Remember…you already have everything you need to get what you want.

~Dr. Barbara L. Swinney

From the Author

...And this is my WHY!

In a period of six months, I got a divorce, experienced a significant shift in my career as a leader, bought a house, sold a house, sent a child off to college, and started a life and leadership coaching business to help women in leadership, like me, transition through life changing events. All of this in the middle of experiencing the roller coaster ride of my own healing process, and fastening the seat belts of my two daughters as they navigated their new reality. ...And nobody in could help me. No one was there to hold the space for me to think about my "next" while I experienced the turbulence of my "now". I trusted no one and had very little confidence that I would be given grace should my performance fall below the level of excellence to which I had been accustomed.

Leaders are often invincible in the eyes of those we lead. To take a knee to life's challenges and tip your hat to leadership could be detrimental to your career. So, we suffer in silence. With smiles plastered on our faces, we put on our heels or best suits and we walk; we keep moving—we do what we are gifted and paid to do. We lose ourselves under the pressure of being what we are expected to be.

This is not just my story. This is the story of many leaders that I have encountered; and this is my why. This is why I am passionate about helping leaders transition through life changing events while balancing the demands of leadership. This is why I am here to help you become a DEEPER Leader!

As a Certified Life and Leadership Coach, author, speaker, and trainer with more than 20 years of leadership experience, I have faced quite a few personal and professional challenges along the way. Through it all, I have learned that many of the difficult experiences I have had were to prepare me for YOU. I went through it all so that I could be there to hold the space for you to think about your "NEXT" while experiencing the turbulence of your "NOW"; to arm you with the strategies necessary to achieve perpetual success in every area of your life; to help you live The DEEPER Life®! I have learned to live my purpose from any position and achieve my personal and professional goals. Now, my goal is to help you do the same.

Through my Life and Leadership Coaching and Mentoring Programs, I will help you navigate the challenges of life while it happens right in the middle of your leadership! My coaching, mentoring, speaking, and leader development services are sure to inspire you to your "NEXT" and transform your "NOW"!

My name is Dr. Barbara Swinney, and I, am here to serve!

28170119R00076

Made in the USA
Columbia, SC
06 October 2018